LAWS OF THE CHURCH

Chlothar III,

King of Franks

Translated by: D.P. Curtin

Dalcassian
Publishing
Company

PHILADELPHIA, PA

ISBN: **978-1-960069-75-7** (Paperback)

Library of Congress Control Number:
Author: Curtin, D.P. (1985-)

Front cover image: Weighing the Saddles before Clothar III, Pere Nunyes, Museu Nacional d'Art de Cataluyna
Printed by Ingram Content Group, 1 Ingram Blvd, La Vergne, Tennessee

First printing edition 2020.

Introduction

These five edicts are what remain (in sometime fragmentary form) of the privileges granted to the church by the Merovingian king, Chlothar III. In the annals of French history his reign is not particularly significant. During his tenure the grasp on centralized power continued to deteriorate into the hand of the Mayor of the Palace. Within two generations the Merovingian dynasty would be largely obsolete, and the Carolingian house would seize dominance over French politics.

Some of this can be observed in these documents, where the Mayor of the Palace is named, something unthinkable even earlier on in the century. Moreover, the authority of the forthcoming Carolingian dynasty is one that was built on a powerful alliance with the French church, and with the See of Rome. Chlothar, by granting additional ecclesiastical license to the Mayor of the Palace, would inevitably be signing the death warrant for his own dynasty.

D.P. Curtin
February 21, 2020
Glen Mills, PA

I. Diploma [of Chlothar III] in which two parts of the town of Tauricciaci, are granted to the church of Saint Dionysius, as a public notice - in the year of Our Lord 658.

[Chlothar] king of the Franks, a righteous man [...] We would be rescinded, or we would be rescinded by the judgment of the just, and there, coming to the activity of the monastery of our special patron, St. Dionis, where his precious body has rested. Ingober [...] sup [...] He gave money in reply, that he lived in such a state of affairs, just as Ermelenus himself had given him the very villages of his friends. Yet, the agent himself, on the contrary [...] and the aforesaid priest stood by him, and showed the precariousness made by that very scum, when it was left. It was found that the very scum from the whole of the body [...] with the body of the faculty he had done himself to Ermeleno. However, the agent of the aforementioned basilica took revenge. As for the precarious one from Ermeleno, he went with Chuglibert the German. [...] they must be shown [...] he had written about everybody in his ability, and they themselves were shown to be listed in the present, and they intended that they should be divided into two parts from the aforesaid towns of Tauricciaco and [...] he would be able to claim the said towns and the adjoining lands in his entire possession. For this reason, let us agree with our superiors that we decided to separate the two parts from the pred [...] , while also the wicked man Chadoloald, the count of our palace. [...] because it is thus denounced that this cause, or that which was investigated by the order, has been defended, we order that the same [...] by the kiss of St. Dionis that [...] let them at all times have vengeance. And let there be an abrupt ending of things between them about this matter afterwards.

Theobertus rog [...] November [...] or [...] the third of our kingdom [successfully in the name of the Lord].

II. The diploma by which Clothar, having given several towns to the monastery of St. Dionysius, to be restored by Bishop Beracharius, pronounces the case heard - in the year of Our Lord 658.

[Chlotarius] king of the Franks, inl [...] at Siniscalcis Vuidrachado and Ansbert, the referenda, and Chadoloaldo, the count of our palace, where to sit down to hear the cases of all, or to hold a just judgment, and there coming the agent of the monastery, St. Dioninse, where the precious lord himself rests in body. They asserted against the apostolic man Lord Beracharios the bishop, because Ermelenus once, or his son Goddo in ger[...] to contradict the treasurer [...] it must, which Beracharius said on the contrary. Yet, by the fact that a letter of donation had been written by Ermelenus himself in his genealogy, and because of this the inheritance itself had reached the same. In the present, our ancestors acting for St. Dioninse, by the law of the famous memory of our lord Chlodovia, and his genealogy. Once the king brought forth to be recounted, where [...] Ermeleno [...] Mab [...] exceptions contained, as where and when [...] Ermelenus had done in Beroald and his heirs, they were found to remain empty, and they were to no effect. Yet, wherever the aforementioned Ermelenus, or his son Goddo, wished to give or abandon their faculty, they should have free discretion with the permission of the aforesaid prince. As long as they [...] would be and of h [...]. Now, to recall the dominion [...]on the part of Beracharius, the bishop, out of his own capacity, without repetition, the agent of the aforesaid monastery ought to recall to his own right. In the present our judgments, both parties, for the trampled suit, have been duly accepted. While they were intent on the actual causation, coming from pro [...] a man by the name of Madroaldus, to the above-mentioned men present [...] that of the aforesaid [...] do the above [...] he gave the places to her husband Madroald [...] but in the present it is professed that he had torn up the villages themselves by the title of revenge, having received his own money. It was written that the agent of the holy St. Dioninus asserted at the present time that he wished to receive those two parts of the aforesaid towns which Beracharius had sold. In so far as the righteous man Chadoloaldus the count, ours to us [...] without rep [...] which heirs or [...] the agent of St. Dioninse has to claim the villages, that is: Simplicciaco, Tauriaco, Stupellas, Flaviniaco, Pociusciniaco, Vassurecurti, Burgonno, Alintummas, Sastivale, Cambariaco, Bursiaco, Coriaco and Munciaco. As well as those located in the villages of: Cinnomannico, Andicavo, Rodonuo and Musfa. Hence for the sake of Chagialbert once, and Ermeleno ads [...] prescribed the towns of: Simplicciaco, Tauriaco, Stupellas, Flaviniaco, Pociusciniaco, Vassurecurti, Burgonno, Alintummas, Sastivale, Cambariaco, Bursiaco, Coriaco, and Munsiaco, which by our [...] that Beracharius may be held in the villages themselves, having examined his letter of this meritorious part of the holy St. Dionis or [...] to do and [...] said [...] lord Beracharius. Those two parts [...] It was decided to restore the parts of the monastery in the same way as before [...] and he exposed himself, as at all times, to any slander or repetition of any kind. [...] Madro

III. Diploma [of Clothar III] by which a dispute is resolved in the palace concerning a certain villa given to Erchinoald the Mayor of the Palace, which his son Leudesius had possessed, between the church of Rothomagens and the monastery of St. Dionysius - in the year of Our Lord 659.

[Clotharius, king of the Franks, a righteous man. When we] [...] Vuarattone, Baseno, with the gravines, also Amalberto, Madelando, the old footman, and Vuaningo, the count of the palace, we would stay, and there for the present [...]lation of the actors of the holy Church of Rotominse against five [...] to the holy churches of Rotominse [...] by their letters they had delegated after [...] those who would hold [...] from [...] or the aforesaid actors. [...] they said they would pay. Yet, when they inquired into their instruments, they found that that portion, that is, of the town itself, which from [...] it was this that Erchenoald had once contributed to the Mayor of the Palace. Leudesius himself was in charge of that half of the order [...] have [...] to [...] in the first order [...] among themselves, as it is fitting for priests, with carelessness they ought to divide among themselves equally the debts of the basilica. At the present it is known that they have met in such a way [...] as [...] all their merits or their appurtenances, together with lands, houses, buildings, m [...] pastures or [...] to the basilica of St. Dioninus without repetition [...] Bishop Audoinus, or his successors of the Church of Rotominse with [...] naming [...] you want [...] herself [...] they are able to possess half of the land [...] whence [...] of God

IV. Diploma by which Chlothar grants the town of Corbeia and others to the monastery of Saints Peter and Paul, in a place called Corbeia, on the river called Somma - in the year of Our Lord 659.

Chlothar, king of the Franks, a righteous man. We believe that our reward in the name of God belongs in whatever we give to the holy places for the salvation of the soul, so that it may prosper there perpetually, and we may deserve to have the glory of helping God. Therefore, while we and our noble house, the queen of Baldechild, a monastery in honor of Saints Peter and Paul, the apostles, and Saint Stephen the proto-martyr, on the river Somna, in a place called Corbeia, which Guntland once possessed and came to our treasury, where the venerable man Theodefridus Abbot presides, for the eternal view of God, ordered that the monks should live there under the holy rule. Let your diligence know that we have the whole town of Corbeia, with its adjacencies in its entirety, or other towns including: Folieto, Gentilla, Cipiliaco, Fortilca-Villa, or the rest of their adjacencies in their entirety. And also, Albiniaco with their adjacencies or appendages, as much as our treasury held there, in their entirety in the village of Ambianense, or also Monciaco, Walliaco, Bellirino, with their adjacencies in the village of Atra vatense. Indeed, and the town called the Temple of Mars, situated in the village of Ambianense, in its entirety, with a cord of wood from our forest in Windegonia, that is, through the places named, from the end of Cartainse to the Dominican lake, through the Derude of Siccas, through the Marcasius of the deer, through Bagusta, through the public road, as far as Fraudeharius. Similarly, we have been seen to have conceded a portion in the place called Taceaco, which Frodinus of Ursinus purchased at a given price. Which Frodinus himself gave to our treasury as compensation for another matter, in the very village of Ambianense, from the present day, under complete immunity, without the entry of the judges. Accordingly, by this precept we decree that it shall remain so that both the place of Corbeia itself and the above-mentioned towns, together with lands, houses, manors, buildings, vineyards, forests, meadows, pastures, mills, and all the appurtenances, or what seems to be attached thereto, may be part of the monastery itself or any congregation of the monastery itself may possess or rule. And none of the judges, nor to the monastery itself, nor to his men, nor to his courts, whatsoever we have contributed there since the present day, and that which has been contributed there by us or by successive lords, kings, or by God-fearing men, neither to hear cases, nor to demand relief, nor to make mansions, nor to require preparations, nor any redhibition in the above-named towns, whatever appears to possess at the present time. Or for that matter, as we have said, if it has been added or delegated there by us, or by succeeding kings, or by men who fear God, the judicial power itself does not presume to enter, but a part of the monastery itself, or every congregation existing there, without the entrance of the judges, as we have said, may be able to possess or be dominated under complete immunity. And in order that this law of ours may obtain firmer strength in the perennial season, we and our noble queen Baldechild, have resolved to confirm it under the seals of our hands.

V. Diploma by which Clothar grants immunity from all taxes to the Corbeian monastery - in the year of Our Lord 660.

Chlothar, king of the Franks, an inglorious man, to all agents both present and future. May your greatness and energy increase your reward and divine insight. He has rendered us such a benefit to the administrators or speakers of the monastery of the men of Corbeia, which our lady and queen Baldechildi built with her work. So much so that whenever the monks, messengers, or disputants of the monastery, in parts of the province, or through the rest of the places, to procure capes or exercise the other opportunities of the monastery itself, or go out to buy cellars in any places or territories or parts. Wherever the toll, pontificate, rotaticum, and other redhibitions our treasury is want to demand from preachers or travel agents, these monks, consistent in the aforesaid monastery of Corbeia, both present and those arriving there in the future, shall have a remission in all and at the same time granted. That is, for the reason that neither we, nor our juniors, nor our successors, at any time, regarding what is contained above, should demand from the monks or the messengers or speakers of the monastery itself, in any places and in any orders presumed to be below the limits of our kingdom. Yet, as it has been inserted above, let the monks of the already mentioned holy congregation of the Corbeia monastery and their ministers have the same benefit, granted and at the same time pardoned from our bountiful generosity, so that the holy congregation itself will rather choose from its own benefit to implore the Lord's mercy for the stability of our kingdom. And in order that this precept may be more firmly established and preserved throughout the ages, we and our noble progenitor the lady of Baldechildi, the greatest queen, resolve to confirm it under our seals.

Ordered by Vitrehadus. The sign of the glorious lord Chlothar the king. The sign of the noble Queen Baldechild.

Given under the 23rd day of December, in the 5th year of our reign, Stirpiniacus. Happily in the name of God.

LATIN TEXT

Praeceptiones ecclesiasticae (Clotarius III Francorum), J. P. Migne

I. Diploma [Clotarii III] quo duae partes villae Tauricciaci, causa cognita, ecclesiae Sancti Dionysii asseruntur (ann. 658). (1277A)

[Chlotarius] rex Francorum, vir inluster . . . . deremendum vel justo judicio termenandum resederemus, ibique venientis acturis monasthirii peculiaris patroni nostri domni Dioninse, ubi ipse preciosus in corpore requiisset, Ingober. . . . sup. . . . fimena dedit in respunsis, quod acta conposcio talem habibat, qualiter ipsas villas ipse Ermelenus jocalis suos ei contullerat; sed ipse agentis econtra . . . . et predictus pontefex in presenti adstabat, et precaria ostendebat ab ipsa fimena facta, quo relicta, inventum est quod ipsa fimena de omne corpore . . . . corpore facultatis (1277B)ipsius Ermeleno fecisse: sed agentis predicti basilice vindicione, vel precario ab ipso Ermeleno in germano suo Chugliberctus . . . . conscripta ostend . . . . de omne corpore facultati sui conscripserat, et ipsas (1278A)in presenti ostendedirunt recensendas, et intendibant, quod ipsas duas partis de predictas villas Tauricciaco et . . . . dictas villas adgaecenciasque aearum in integrum suo dominio valeret vendecare. Propterea nus una cum nostris procerebus constet decrevisse, ut ipsas duas partis de pred . . . , dum et inluster vir Chadoloaldus, comis palatii nostri . . . . quod taliter hac causa acta, vel per ordeni inquisita, seo defenita fuisse denuscetur, jubemus ut ipsas . . . . domni Dioninse bactu . . . . que . . . . omni tempore habiant evendecatas, et sit inter ipsis de hac re in postmodum subita causacio.

Teoberctus rog . . . . Novembr. . . . an . . . . rigni nostri tercio [in nomine Domini feliciter].

II. Diploma quo Clotarius villas plures monasterio Sancti Dionysii donatas, a Berachario episcopo restituendas, causa audita pronuntiat (ann. 658). (1278B) [Chlotarius] rex Francorum, V. inl . . . . Siniscalcis (1279A)Vuidrachado et Anseberctho referendariis, et Chadoloaldo, comiti palatii nostro, ad universorum causas audiendum, vel recto judicio termenando resederemus, ibique venientes agentis monasthirii domni Dioninse, ubi ipse preciosus domnus in corpore requiiscit, adversus apostolico viro domno Berachario episcopo adserebant, eo quod Ermelenus quondam, vel filius suos Goddo in ger. . . . erachario contradicere . . . . debet, qui Beracharius econtra dicebat, eo quod ab ipso Ermeleno in geniture suo exinde epistola donationis fuisse conscripta, et ob hoc ipsa heredetas ad eodem pervenissit: sed in presenti antefati agentis domni Dioninse precepcione incliti recordationis domni et genituris nostri Chlodoviei, quondam regis protullerunt recensenda, ubi . . . . (1279B)Ermeleno . . . . (Mab. . . . . eceptio) contenibat, ut ubi et ubi ille . . . . Ermelenus in Beroaldo heredebusque suis ficerat, invenibantur vacuas et inanis permansirent, et nullum sortirentur effectum; sed ubicumque antedictus Ermelenus vel filius suos Goddo eorum facultatem dare aut derelinquere vellibant, liberum ex permisso predicto princepe habirent arbitrium. Sed dummodo inter se fo . . . . (foret) et de h . . . . iat (desunt apud Mabill.) revocare dominium . . . . parti Beracharius episcopus ex ipsa facultate absque repeticionem agentum predicti monasthirii ad suum jure revocare deberit: quod et in presenti judicia nostra utrasque partis pro calcada (Mab. calcanda) lite, vise fuerunt accepisse. Sed dum in ipsa causacione intenderent, veniens ex pro . . . . homo, nomene (1279C)Madroaldus, presentebus suprascriptis viris . . . . quod de predict. . . . fecere suprascr. . .., loca Madroaldo viro dedissit . . . . sed in presenti professus est, quod ipsas villas per vindicionis titolum, accepta sua pecunia distraxerat; suprascript. agentis sancti domni Dioninse in presenti asserebant quod illas duas partes de predictis villabus, quod Beracharius vindedirat, recipire vellibat. Sed in quantum inluster vir Chadoloaldus, comis pal. nostri nobis . . . . absque rep . . . . que heredebus vel . . . . seo agentis domni Dioninse habeat, evindicaret in villas, id sunt, Simplicciaco, Tauriaco, Stupellas, Flaviniaco, Pociusciniaco, Vassurecurti, Burgonno, Alintummas, Sastivale, Cambariaco, Bursiaco, Coriaco et Munciaco sitas in pagus Cinnomannico, Andicavo, Rodonuo (1279D)(Mab. Rodonico) et Musfa: unde in causacionem (1280A)pro Chagilbertho quondam et Ermeleno ads . . . . prescrip. villas Simplicciaco, Tauriaco, Stupellas, Flaviniaco, Pociusciniaco, Vassurecurti, Burgonno, Alintummas, Sastivale, Cambariaco, Bursiaco, Coriaco et Munsiaco, quem per nostro . . . . quod in ipsas villas Beracharius habire poterit, inspecta sua epistola hujus mereti partibus sancti domni Dioninse vel . . . . facire et . . . .

dictum . . . . domnus Beracharius. (Hic aliquot puncta apud Mab.) Illas duas partis . . . . partibus monasthirii placuit restaurare semileter antefa . . . . et expopondedit ut omni tempore, se alequa calumnia aut repeticionem quislib. . . . Madro.

III. Diploma [Clotarii III] quo lis in palatio dirimitur de quadam villa Erchinoaldo majori-domus collata, quam filius ejus Leudesius possederat, inter ecclesiam Rothomagensem et monasterium Sancti Dionysii (ann. 659). (1280B) [Clotharius, rex Francorum, vir inluster. Cum nos] . . . . . Vuaratttone, Baseno, gravionibus, item Amalberto, Madelando, seniscalcis, et Vuaningo, comite palatii, resederemus, ibique in praesentia . . . . latione actores sancti Aecclesie Rotominse adversus V . . . . ad sancta Aecclisia Rotominse . . . . per eorum epistolas delegaverant post . . . . tenerent inlebete qui . . . . ab . . . . vel actores antedicti . . . . dicebant reddebere. Sed inquirentes eorum instrumenta, invenerunt quod illa porcio, hoc est de ipsa villa quod a . . . . erat hoc Erchenoaldo quondam majorem-domus (1280C)contulerat: et ipse Leudesius ligetemo ordene illa medietate . . . . habe . . . . ad . . . . ordene pri . . . . inter se, sicut decet sacerdotes, cum caretate inraciones ad basileca inter se aequaliter devidere deberint. Quod et in praesenti taliter noscitur convenisse . . . . ut . . . . omni mereto vel adjecentias suas, una cum terris, domibus, aedificies, m . . . . pascuis vel . . . . ad basilica domni Dionynse absque repeticione . . . . Audoino episcopo, vel successores suos Ecclesiae Rotominse cu . . . . nomenante . . . . vis . . . . ipsa . . . . loca medietate valeant possedere . . . . unde . . . . Dei.

IV. Diploma quo Clotarius villam Corbeiam et alias confert monasterio Sanctorum Petri et Pauli, in loco qui dicitur Corbeia, super fluvium qui vocatur Somma (ann. 659). (1280D)Chlotharius, rex Francorum, vir inluster. Ad mercedem (1281A)nostram in Dei nomine credimus pertinere, quicquid pro animae salute locis sanctorum conferimus, ut ibidem perenniter proficiat, et gloriam, Deo auxiliante, habere mereamur. Igitur dum nos et praecelsa genetrix nostra, domna Baldechildis regina, monasterium in honore sanctorum Petri et Pauli, apostolorum, et sancti Stephani, proto-martyris, super fluvium Somna, in loco qui dicitur Corbeia, quem Guntlandus quondam possederat, et ad fiscum nostrum pervenerat, ubi praeest venerabilis vir Theodefridus abba, pro aeterni numinis intuiti aedificari praecepimus, ut monachi sub sancta regula ibidem debeant conversari. Cognoscat strenuitas vestra quod nos ipsam villam Corbeiam ad ipsum monasterium, cum adjacentiis suis in integrum, seu et alias villas (1281B)nuncupantes Folieto, Gentilla, Cipiliaco, Fortilca-Villa, vel reliquas adjacentias earum ad integrum, Albiniaco cum adjacentiis vel appenditiis suis, quantum ibidem fiscus noster tenuit, ad integrum in pago Ambianense, seu et Monciaco, Walliaco, Bellirino, cum adjacentiis earum in pago Atravatense: immoque et villam quae vocatur Templum Martis, sitam in pago Ambianense, ad integrum, cum pagena de silva de foreste nostra Windegonia, hoc est, per loca denominata, a fine Cartainse usque in dominico lacco, per Siccasi derude, per cervorum Marcasio, per Bagusta, per via publica, usque Fraudehario exsarto. Similiter et portionem in loco qui vocatur Taceaco, quem Frodinus de Ursino dato pretio comparavit, et ad fiscum nostrum ipse Frodinus in compensationem (1281C)pro alia re dedit, in ipso pago Ambianense, a die praesenti, sub integra immunitate, absque introitu judicum, visi fuimus concessisse. Proinde per hanc praeceptionem specialius decernimus esse mansurum ut, tam ipsum locum Corbeiam quam et suprascriptas villas, una cum terris, domibus, mancipiis, aedificiis, vineis, silvis, pratis, pascuis, farinariis, et cunctis appenditiis, vel quod ibidem videtur adspicere, pars ipsius monasterii vel omnis congregatio de ipso monasterio valeat possidere vel dominari. Et nullus quilibet de judicibus, nec ad ipsum monasterium, nec ad homines suos, nec in curtes suas, quicquid a die praesenti ibidem contulimus, et quod a nobis vel a succedentibus domnis regibus, vel a (1281D)Deum timentibus hominibus inibi fuerit collatum, nec ad causas audiendum, nec freda exigendum, nec mansiones faciendum, nec paratas requirendum, nec (1282A)ullas redhibitiones in villis superius nominatis, quidquid tempore praesenti videtur possidere, aut adhuc, ut diximus, a nobis vel a succedentibus regibus, vel a Deum timentibus hominibus inibi additum vel delegatum fuerit, ipsa judiciaria potestas non praesumat ingredi, sed pars ipsius monasterii vel omnis congregatio ibidem consistens, absque introitu judicum, ut diximus, sub integra immunitate possidere valeat vel dominari. Et ut haec praeceptio nostra perenni tempore firmiorem obtineat vigorem, nos et praecelsa genetrix nostra Baldechildis regina, signaculis manus nostrae subter decrevimus affirmare.

V. Diploma quo Clotarius immunitatem ab omni teloneo concedit monasterio Corbeiensi (ann. 660). (1282B)Chlotharius, rex Francorum, vir inluster, omnibus agentibus tam praesentibus quam futuris. Cognoscat magnitudo seu industria vestra, pro mercedis vestrae augmento et divino intuitu, tale nos actoribus seu discursoribus monasterii virorum Corbeia, quod domna et genetrix nostra Baldechildis regina suo opere construxit, praestitisse beneficium, ut quotienscumque monachi, missi, vel discussores ipsius monasterii, partibus provinciae, vel per reliqua loca, ad cappas comparandas aut reliquas opportunitates ipsius monasterii exercendum, seu cellarium fuerint egressi mercandum in quibuslibet locis vel territoriis seu partibus, ubicumque teloneum, pontaticum, rotaticum, ceterasque redhibitiones fiscus noster a discursoribus, seu iter agentibus exigere consuevit, (1282C)habeant hoc monachi in jam dicto monasterio Corbeia consistentes, tam praesentes quam in futurum inibi advenientes, in omnibus indultum simulque concessum. Ea scilicet ratione ut neque nos, neque juniores, aut successores nostri, ullo unquam tempore, de eo quod superius continetur, a monachis aut missis vel discursoribus ipsius monasterii exigere nec requirere, ullis locis ullisque ordinibus infra terminos regni nostri praesumatis. Sed ut super habetur insertum, habeant ipsum beneficium jam dicti monachi sanctae congregationis Corbeia monasterio et actores eorum, ex nostrae largitatis munificentia concessum simulque indultum, quo potius delectet ipsam sanctam congregationem ex ipso beneficio pro (1282D)stabilitate regni nostri Domini misericordiam exorare. Et ut haec praeceptio firmior habeatur et per tempora conservetur, nos et praecelsa genetrix nostra (1283A)domna Baldechildis, regina maxima, nostris signaculis subter eam decernimus adfirmare. Vidrehadus jussus. Signum gloriosi domni Chlotarii regis. (1284A)Signum praecelsae Baldechildis reginae. Data sub die XXIII mensis Decembris, anno V regni nostri, Stirpiniaco. In Dei nomine feliciter.

The Scriptorium Project is the work of a small group of lay people of various apostolic churches who are interested in the preservation, transmission, and translation of the works of the early and medieval church. Our efforts are to make the works of the church fathers accessible to anyone who might have an interest in Christian antiquities and the theological, philosophical, and moral writings that have become the bedrock of Western Civilization.

To-date, our releases have pulled from the Greek, Syriac, Georgian, Latin, Celtic, Ethiopian, and Coptic traditions of Christianity, and have been pulled from sundry local traditions and languages.

Other Titles and Translations by D.P. Curtin:

First Book of Ethiopian Maccabees (2018)
Protoevangelium of James: Greek and English Texts (2019)
Edicts of the Synod of Paris by Chlothar II, King of Franks (2019)
The Life of St. Desiderius by Sisebut, King of Visigoths (2019)
The Synod of Rome by St. Boniface IV of Rome (2019)
Letter to Pope Theodore by Victor of Carthage (2020)
The Decree of 610 by Gundemar, King of Visigoths (2020)
Laws of the Church by Chlothar III, King of Franks (2020)
Donations by St. Aethelbert, King of Kent (2020)
The Mystical Interpretation by St. Aileran the Wise (2020)
Laws of the Church by St. Dagobert II, King of Franks (2020)
The Old Nubian Miracle of St. Mena (2021)
About Fifteen Problems by St. Albertus Magnus (2022)
Testament of Some Former Things by John Scotus Eriugena (2022)
The Georgian Synaxarium (2022)
Instructions: Counsel for Novices by St. Ammonas the Hermit (2022)
The Syriac Menologium and Martyrology (2022)
Book on Religious Exercise and Quiet by St. Isaiah the Solitary (2022)
Vision of Theophilus by St. Cyril of Alexandria (2022)
On Fate (De Fato) by St. Albertus Magnus (2023)
Fragments of 'Chronicle' by Hippolytus of Thebes (2023)
Life of the Blessed Theotokos by Epiphanius Monachus (2023)
Syriac Life of John the Baptist by Serapion the Presbyter (2023)
Second Book of Ethiopian Maccabees (2023)

www.ingramcontent.com/pod-product-compliance
Lightning Source LLC
Chambersburg PA
CBHW070958120626

46546CB00004B/1671